Alfred's Basic Piano Library

Piano

Ensemble Book · Level 1B

NINE 4-PART ENSEMBLES FOR 4 KEYBOARDS

Willard A. Palmer • Morton Manus • Amanda Vick Lethco

Ensembles arranged by

Gayle Kowalchyk • E. L. Lancaster

ENSEMBLE BOOK 1B of Alfred's Basic Piano Library contains 9 four-part ensembles, carefully coordinated PAGE BY PAGE with the material in LESSON BOOK 1B. Part 1 of each ensemble is a selected favorite from FUN BOOK 1B or RECITAL BOOK 1B in its original version. Parts 2, 3 and 4 were written using the same concepts and hand positions at the same level of difficulty. Students will enjoy the rich sounds created by combining the four parts on different keyboards or recording each part on a sequencer.

Each part is notated within the student's reading range on a separate page to facilitate ease in reading. Combined scores for the teacher are located on pages 46–56.

For those students using electronic instruments, suggested electronic sounds are given for each part. These sounds were chosen from a Roland sound module. Students using other instruments will be able to find similar sounds.

The ensembles provide excellent motivational material for group lessons, recitals and monster concerts. Enjoy!

Copyright © MCMXCII by Alfred Publishing Co., Inc.

Illustrations by David Silverman

Music Engraving by Tom Gerou

Use after MONEY CAN'T BUY EV'RYTHING!
LESSON BOOK 1B (page 8).

Part 1 *Suggested Sound*
Organ/Elec Org 4

Will You, Won't You?

C POSITION

Adapted from "Alice in Wonderland,"
by Lewis Carroll

Moderately fast

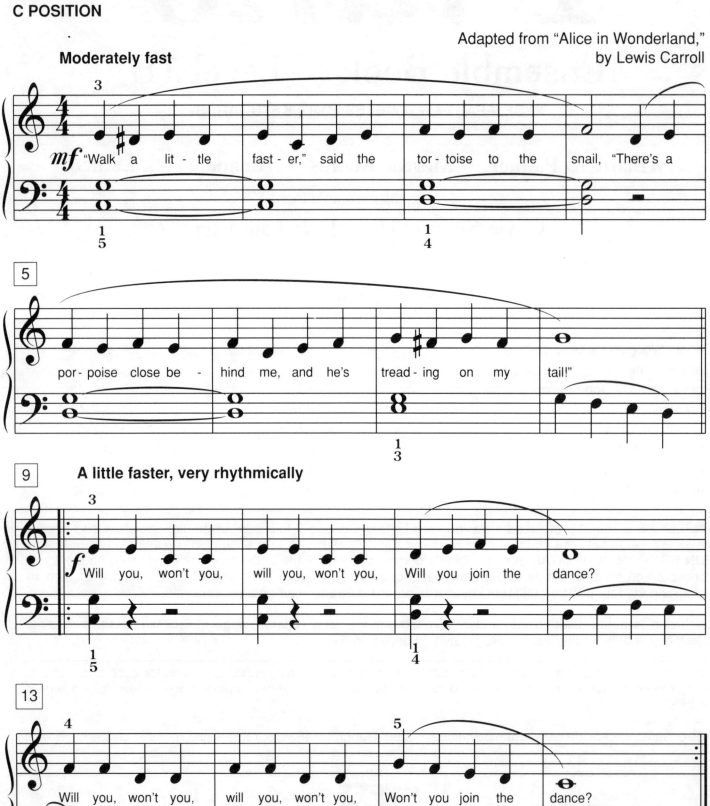

A little faster, very rhythmically

TEACHER: See page 46.

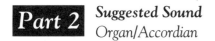

Part 2 *Suggested Sound*
Organ/Accordian

Will You, Won't You?

C POSITION

Moderately fast

A little faster, very rhythmically

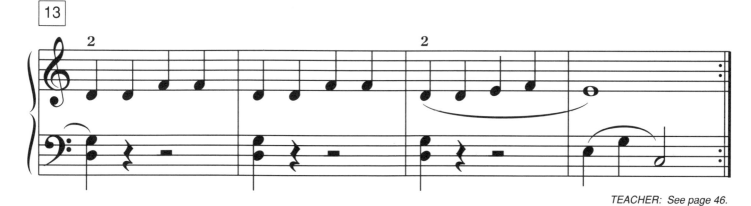

TEACHER: See page 46.

4

Use after MONEY CAN'T BUY EV'RYTHING!
LESSON BOOK 1B (page 8).

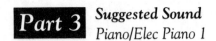

Part 3 *Suggested Sound*
Piano/Elec Piano 1

Will You, Won't You?

C POSITION

Moderately fast

Both hands one octave higher than written throughout

A little faster, very rhythmically

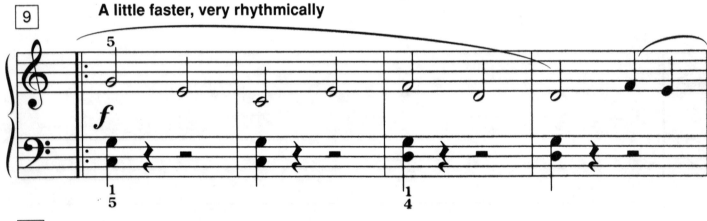

TEACHER: See page 46.

Part 4 *Suggested Sound*
Piano/Honkytonk

Will You, Won't You?

C POSITION

Moderately fast

Both hands one octave lower than written throughout

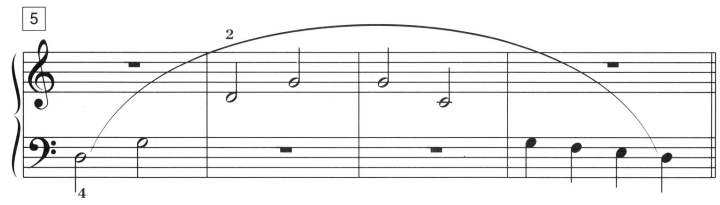

A little faster, very rhythmically

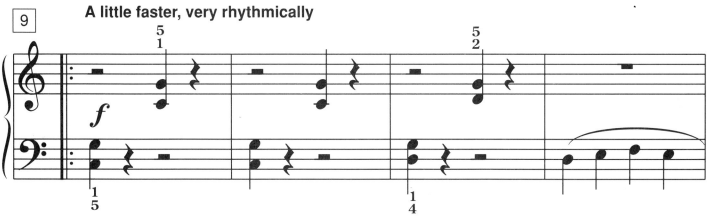

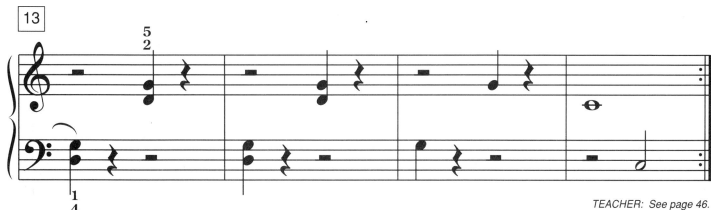

TEACHER: See page 46.

Use after THE CLOWN (page 15).

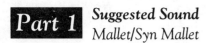

Part 1 *Suggested Sound*
Mallet/Syn Mallet

Hiawatha
G POSITION

Moderato

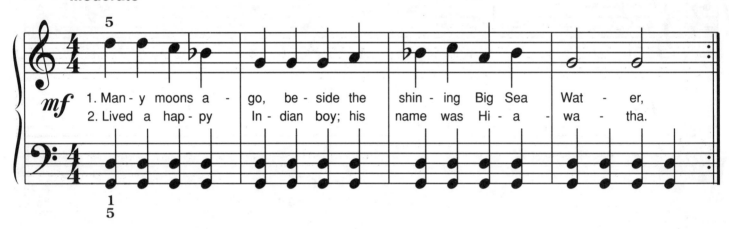

1. Man - y moons a - go, be - side the shin - ing Big Sea Wat - er,
2. Lived a hap - py In - dian boy; his name was Hi - a - wa - tha.

He grew up to be a chief - tan, wise and kind and brave and strong. Think of might - y

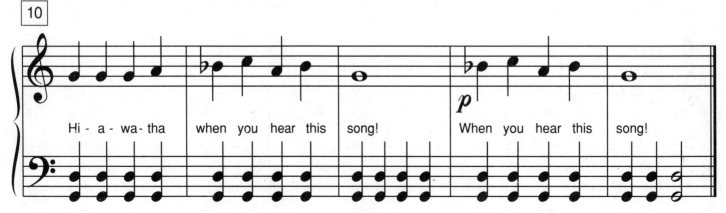

Hi - a - wa - tha when you hear this song! When you hear this song!

TEACHER: *See page 47.*

Part 2 *Suggested Sound*
Mallet/Xylophone

Hiawatha

G POSITION

Moderato

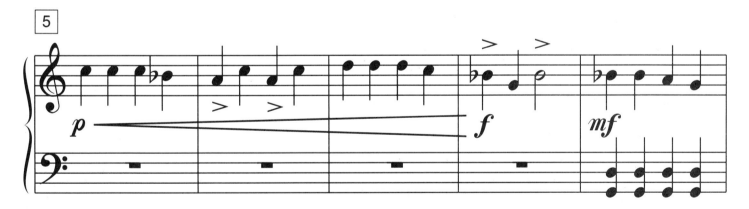

TEACHER: See page 47.

8

Part 3 *Suggested Sound*
Special/Breathpipe

Hiawatha
G POSITION

Moderato

RH one octave higher than written throughout

LH two octaves higher than written throughout

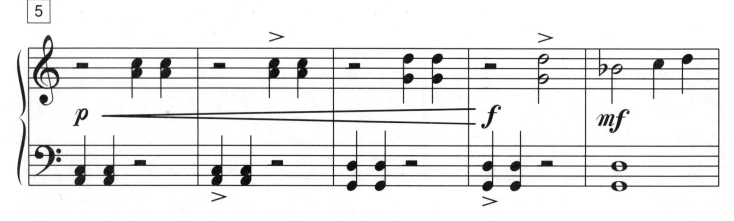

TEACHER: See page 47.

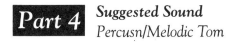

Part 4   *Suggested Sound*
Percusn/Melodic Tom

Hiawatha
G POSITION

Moderato

RH two octaves lower than written throughout

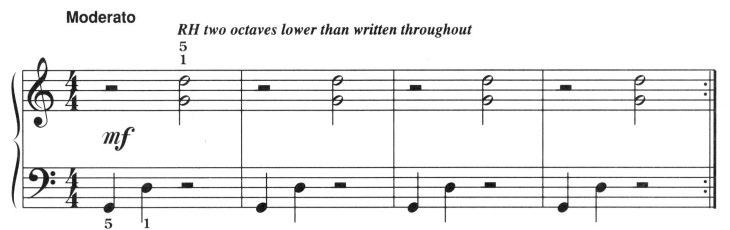

LH one octave lower than written throughout

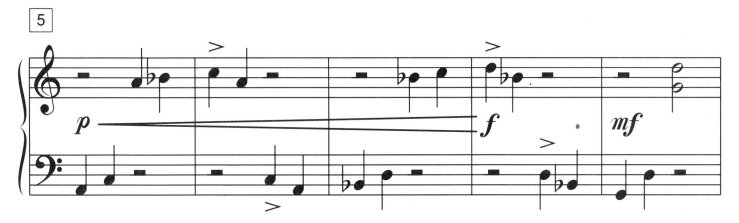

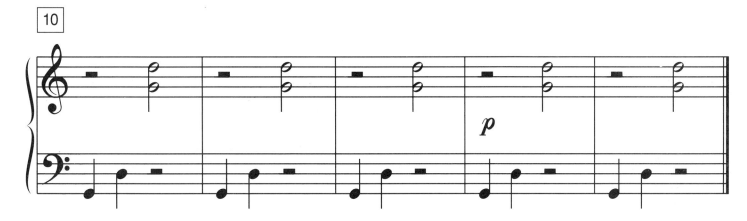

TEACHER: See page 47.

Use after THE RAINBOW (page 19).

Part 1 *Suggested Sound*
Brass/Trombone I

For He's a Jolly Good Fellow!

MIDDLE C POSITION

Pedal optional

TEACHER: See page 48.

Part 2 *Suggested Sound*
Wind 2/Clarinet 1

For He's a Jolly Good Fellow!

MIDDLE C POSITION

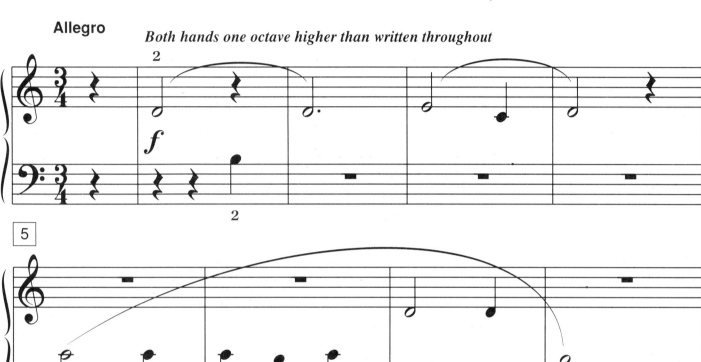

Allegro

Both hands one octave higher than written throughout

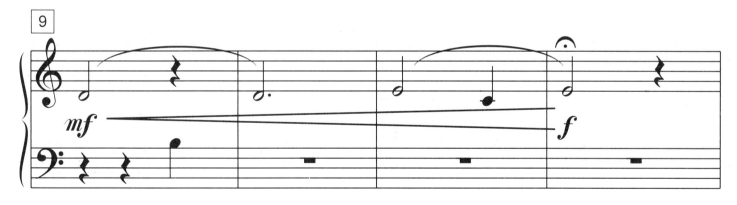

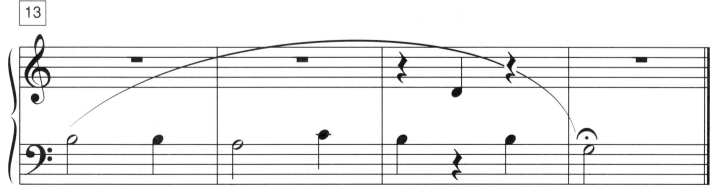

Pedal optional

TEACHER: See page 48.

Use after THE RAINBOW (page 19).

Part 3 *Suggested Sound*
Wind 1/Piccolo 2

For He's a Jolly Good Fellow!

MIDDLE C POSITION

Allegro

Both hands two octaves higher than written throughout

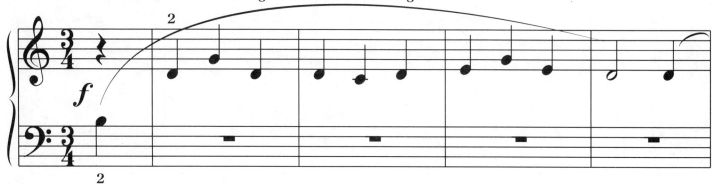

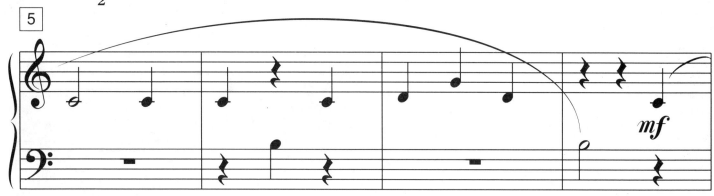

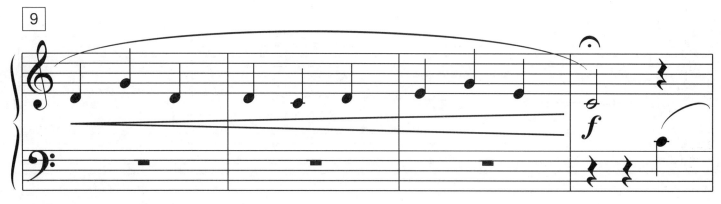

Pedal optional

TEACHER: See page 48.

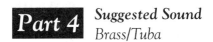

Part 4   *Suggested Sound*
          Brass/Tuba

For He's a Jolly Good Fellow!

MIDDLE C POSITION

Pedal optional

TEACHER: See page 48.

14

Use after HAPPY BIRTHDAY TO YOU! (page 21).

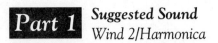

Part 1 *Suggested Sound*
Wind 2/Harmonica

Whoopee Ti-Yi-Yo

C POSITION

Allegro moderato

Cowboy Song

Part 2   *Suggested Sound*
Strings/Violin 1

Whoopee Ti-Yi-Yo

C POSITION

TEACHER: See page 49.

16

Use after HAPPY BIRTHDAY TO YOU! (page 21).

Part 3 *Suggested Sound*
Strings/Pizzicato

Whoopee Ti-Yi-Yo

C POSITION

Allegro moderato

Both hands one octave higher than written throughout

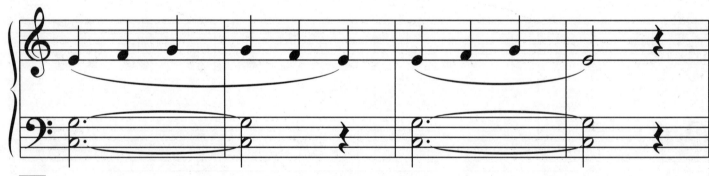

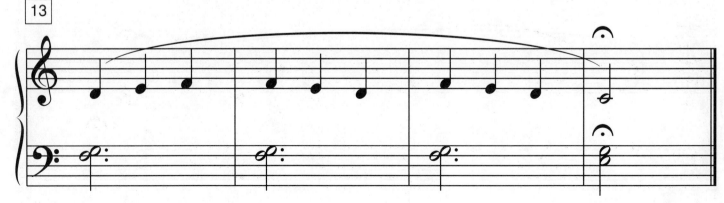

TEACHER: See page 49.

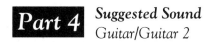

Part 4 *Suggested Sound*
Guitar/Guitar 2

Whoopee Ti-Yi-Yo

C POSITION

Allegro moderato

Both hands one octave lower than written throughout

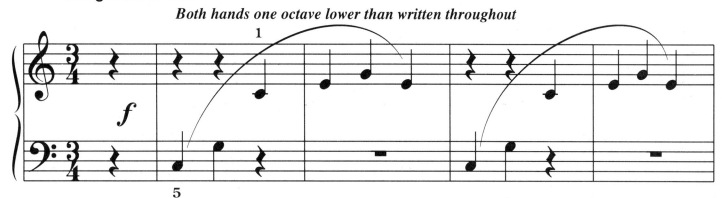

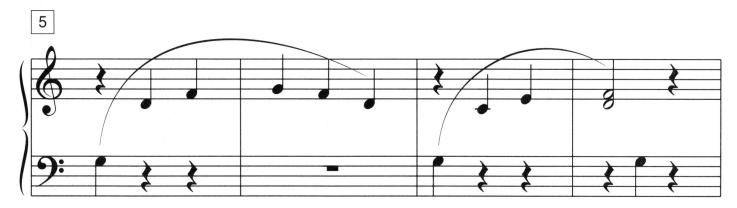

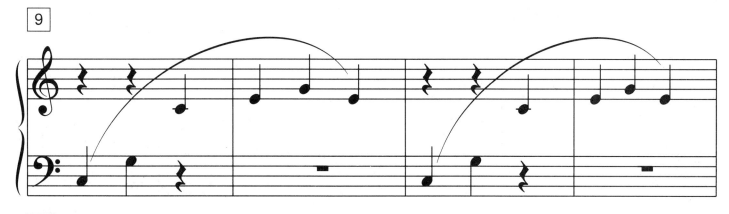

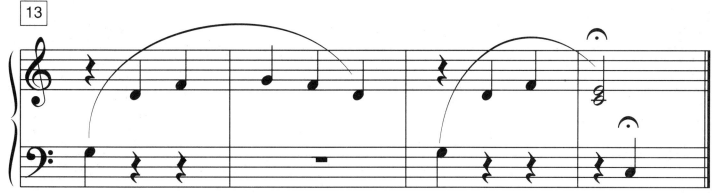

TEACHER: See page 49.

Use after INDIANS (page 24).

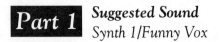

Part 1 *Suggested Sound*
Synth 1/Funny Vox

Barrel of Monkeys!

G POSITION

Happily

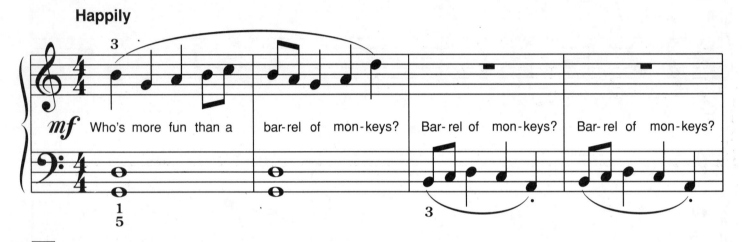

mf Who's more fun than a bar-rel of mon-keys? Bar-rel of mon-keys? Bar-rel of mon-keys?

5

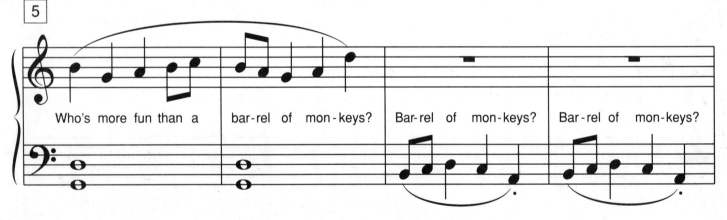

Who's more fun than a bar-rel of mon-keys? Bar-rel of mon-keys? Bar-rel of mon-keys?

9

*Both hands
one octave higher* - - - -
*Both hands
two octaves higher* - - - -
*Both hands
one octave lower* - -

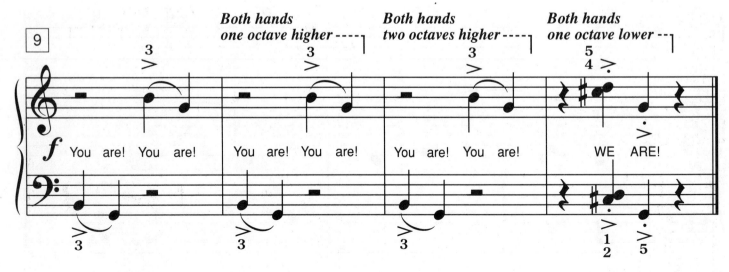

f You are! You are! You are! You are! You are! You are! WE ARE!

TEACHER: See page 50.

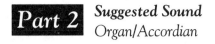

Part 2 *Suggested Sound*
Organ/Accordian

Barrel of Monkeys!

G POSITION

Happily

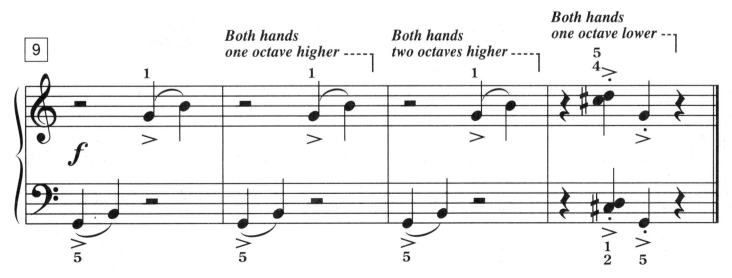

TEACHER: See page 50.

20

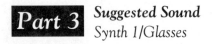 **Part 3** *Suggested Sound*
Synth 1/Glasses

Barrel of Monkeys!

G POSITION

Happily

Both hands two octaves higher than written throughout

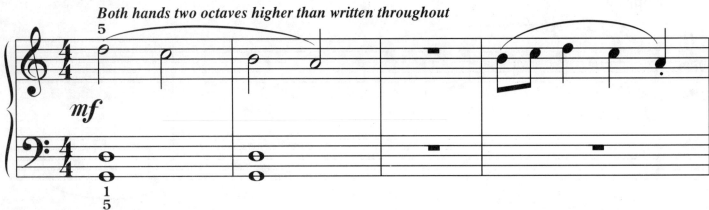

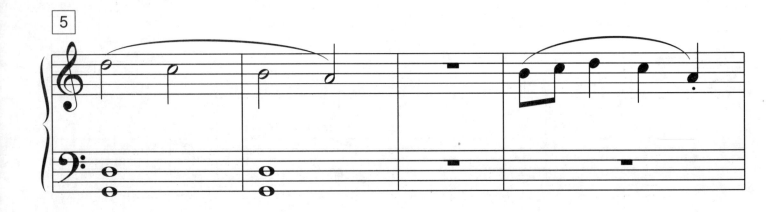

TEACHER: See page 50.

Use after INDIANS (page 24).

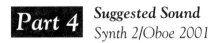 **Part 4** *Suggested Sound*
Synth 2/Oboe 2001

Barrel of Monkeys!

G POSITION

Happily

RH two octaves lower than written throughout

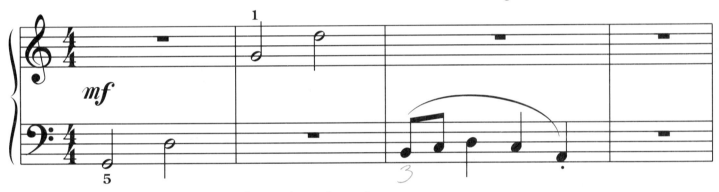

mf

LH one octave lower than written throughout

f

TEACHER: See page 50.

Use after THE MAGIC MAN (page 32).

Part 1 *Suggested Sound*
Wind 2/Sax 2

Boogie-Woogie Goose

C POSITION

Allegro moderato

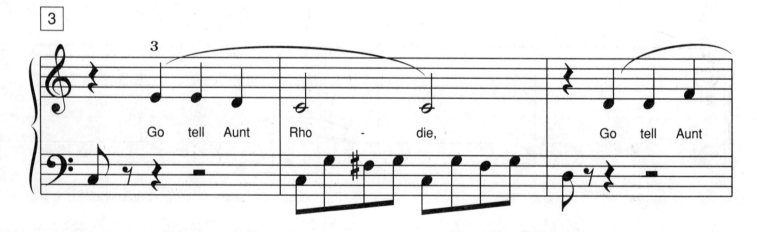

Go tell Aunt Rho - die,   Go tell Aunt

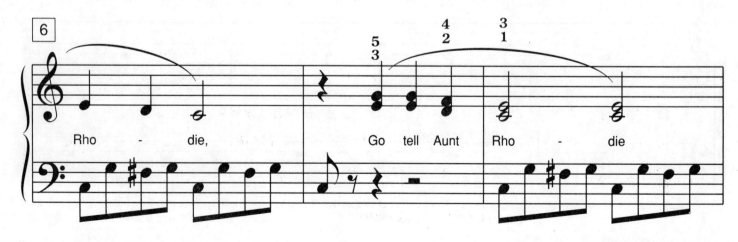

Rho - die,   Go tell Aunt Rho - die

TEACHER: See pages 51–52.

Use after THE MAGIC MAN (page 32).

Part 2 *Suggested Sound*
Wind 2/Clarinet 2

Boogie-Woogie Goose

C POSITION

Allegro moderato

Both hands one octave higher than written throughout

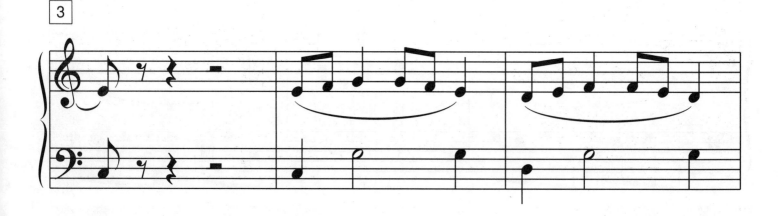

TEACHER: See pages 51–52.

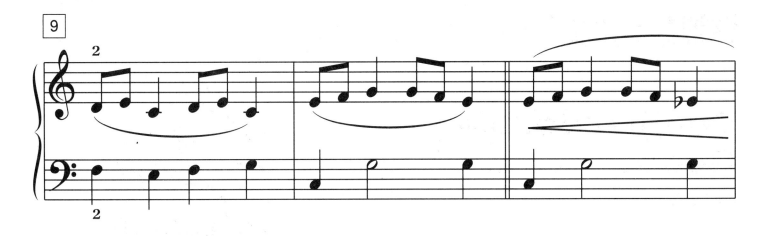

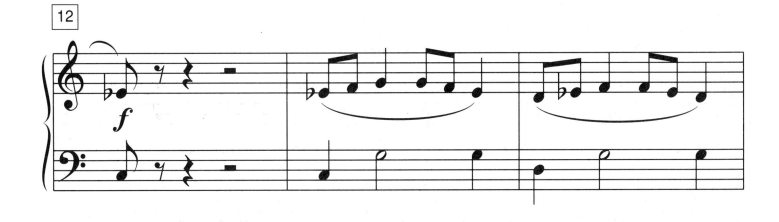

26

Use after THE MAGIC MAN (page 32).

Boogie-Woogie Goose

C POSITION

Allegro moderato

Both hands two octaves higher than written throughout

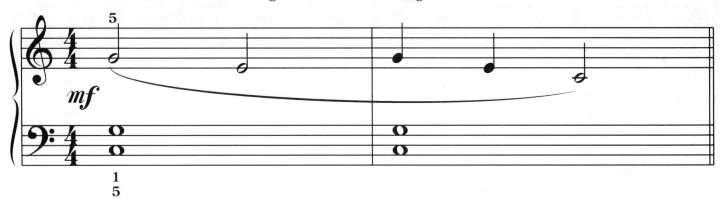

mf

3
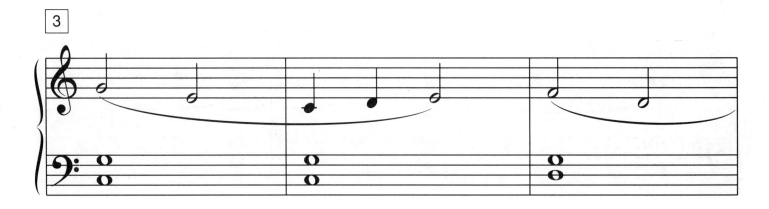

6
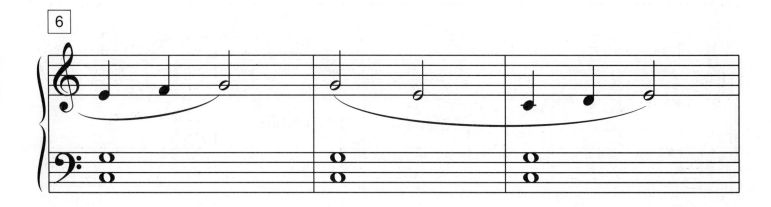

TEACHER: See pages 51–52.

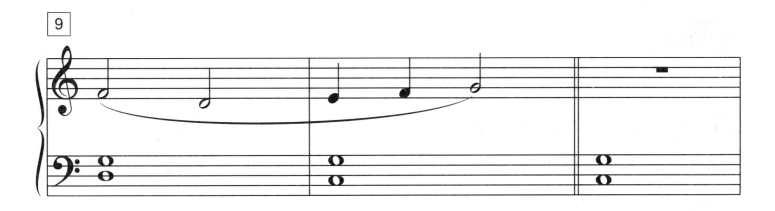

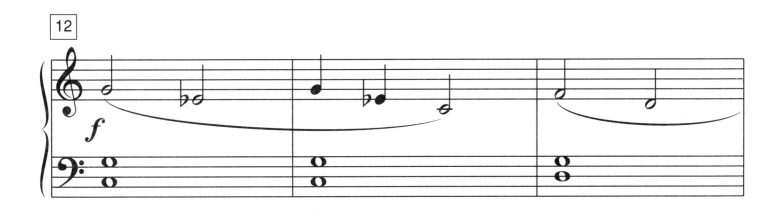

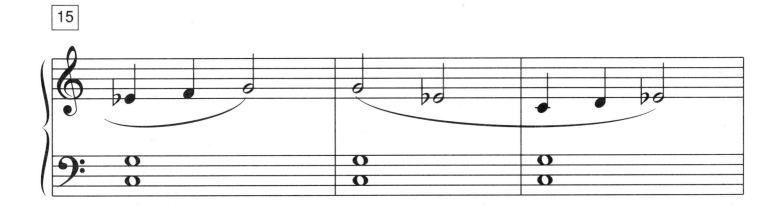

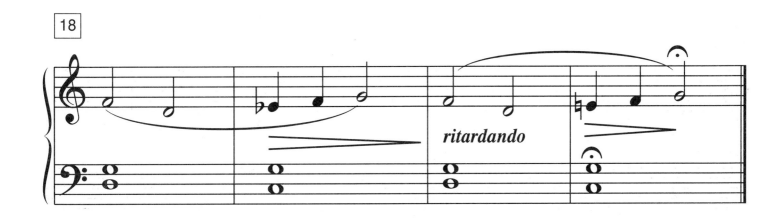

Use after THE MAGIC MAN (page 32).

Suggested Sound
Bass/Slap Bass 1

Boogie-Woogie Goose

C POSITION

Allegro moderato

Both hands one octave lower than written throughout

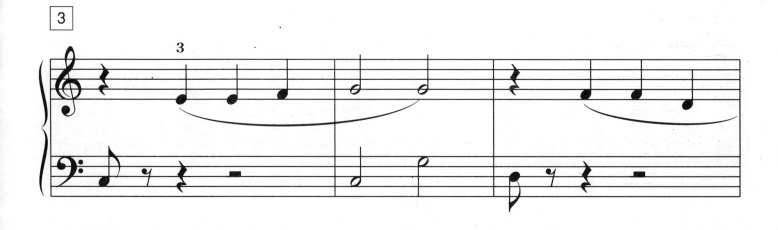

TEACHER: See pages 51–52.

Use after MEASURING HALF STEPS (page 36).

Part 1 *Suggested Sound*
Brass/Trumpet 1

On With the Show!

C POSITION

March tempo

On with the show! Strike up the band! Come on, let's go!

TEACHER: See pages 53–54.

32

Use after MEASURING HALF STEPS (page 36).

Part 2 *Suggested Sound*
Brass/Fr Horn 2

On With the Show!

C POSITION

March tempo

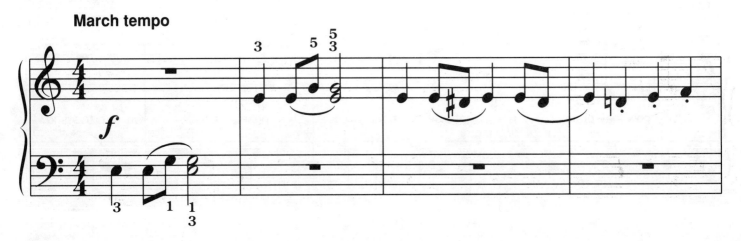

TEACHER: See pages 53–54.

Use after MEASURING HALF STEPS (page 36).

Part 3   *Suggested Sound*
Wind 2/Clarinet 1

On With the Show!

C POSITION

March tempo
Both hands two octaves higher than written throughout

TEACHER: See pages 53–54.

Use after MEASURING HALF STEPS (page 36).

Part 4   *Suggested Sound*
Brass/Trombone 1

On With the Show!

C POSITION

March tempo

Both hands one octave lower than written throughout

TEACHER: See pages 53–54.

38

Use after THE KEY OF G MAJOR (page 42).

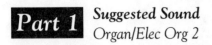

Part 1 *Suggested Sound*
Organ/Elec Org 2

Three Wise Monkeys

KEY OF G MAJOR
Key Signature: 1 sharp (F♯)

HAND POSITION: LH plays lower tetrachord
RH plays upper tetrachord

TEACHER: See page 55.

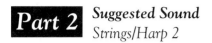 **Part 2** | *Suggested Sound*
Strings/Harp 2

Three Wise Monkeys

KEY OF G MAJOR
Key Signature: 1 sharp (F♯)

HAND POSITION: LH plays lower tetrachord
RH plays upper tetrachord

Allegro moderato

Both hands one octave higher than written throughout

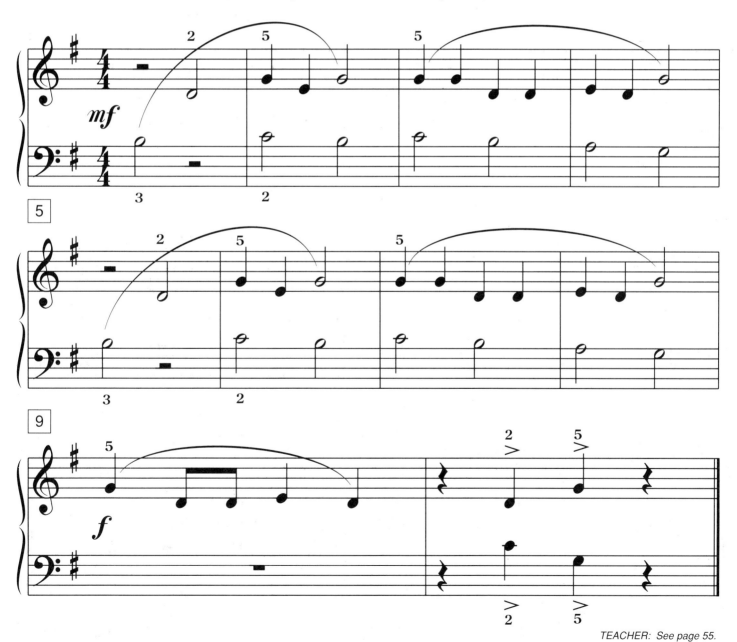

TEACHER: See page 55.

40

Use after THE KEY OF G MAJOR (page 42).

Part 3 *Suggested Sound*
Strings/Pizzicato

Three Wise Monkeys

KEY OF G MAJOR
Key Signature: 1 sharp (F♯)

HAND POSITION: LH plays lower tetrachord
RH plays upper tetrachord

Allegro moderato

Both hands two octaves higher than written throughout

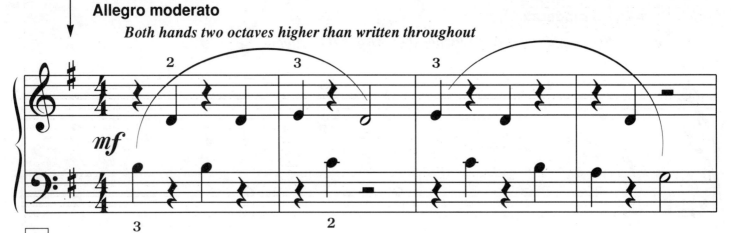

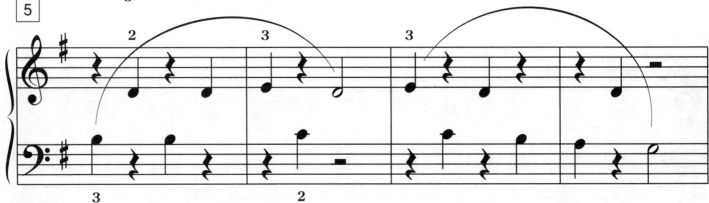

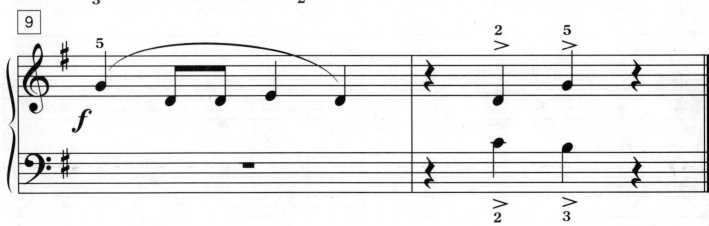

TEACHER: See page 55.

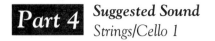

Suggested Sound
Strings/Cello 1

Three Wise Monkeys

KEY OF G MAJOR
Key Signature: 1 sharp (F♯)

HAND POSITION: LH plays lower tetrachord
RH plays upper tetrachord

Allegro moderato

Both hands one octave lower than written throughout

TEACHER: See page 55.

42

*Use after WHEN OUR BAND GOES MARCHING BY! (page 46)
or with the beginning of LESSON BOOK 2.*

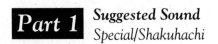

The Caravan

RH: C POSITION
LH: LOW G POSITION

Use after WHEN OUR BAND GOES MARCHING BY! (page 46)
or with the beginning of LESSON BOOK 2.

Part 2 *Suggested Sound*
Special/Koto

The Caravan

RH: C POSITION
LH: LOW G POSITION

Andante moderato

Both hands one octave higher than written throughout

TEACHER: See page 56.

Use after WHEN OUR BAND GOES MARCHING BY! (page 46)
or with the beginning of LESSON BOOK 2.

Part 3   *Suggested Sound*
Special/Whistle 1

The Caravan

RH: C POSITION
LH: LOW G POSITION

Andante moderato

Both hands two octaves higher than written throughout

TEACHER: See page 56.

Use after WHEN OUR BAND GOES MARCHING BY! (page 46)
or with the beginning of LESSON BOOK 2.

Suggested Sound
Special/Bottleblow

The Caravan

RH: C POSITION
LH: LOW G POSITION

Andante moderato

Both hands one octave lower than written throughout

TEACHER: See page 56.

Use after MONEY CAN'T BUY EV'RYTHING!
LESSON BOOK 1B (page 8).

Ensemble Parts 1–4

Suggested Sounds: **Part 1** *Organ/Elec Org 4*   **Part 3** *Piano/Elec Piano 1*

                                    Part 2 *Organ/Accordian*   **Part 4** *Piano/Honkytonk*

Will You, Won't You?

C POSITION

Ensemble Parts 1–4

Suggested Sounds:

Part 1 *Mallet/Syn Mallet* **Part 3** *Special/Breakpipe*

Part 2 *Mallet/Xylophone* **Part 4** *Percusn/Melodic Tom*

Hiawatha

G POSITION

LH one octave lower than written throughout

Use after THE RAINBOW (page 19).

Ensemble Parts 1–4

Suggested Sounds:

Part 1 *Brass/Trombone 1* **Part 3** *Wind 1/Piccolo 2*

Part 2 *Wind 2/Clarinet 1* **Part 4** *Brass/Tuba*

For He's a Jolly Good Fellow!

MIDDLE C POSITION

Ensemble Parts 1–4
Suggested Sounds:

Part 1 *Wind 2/Harmonica*	**Part 3** *Strings/Pizzicato*
Part 2 *Strings/Violin 1*	**Part 4** *Guitar/Guitar 2*

Whoopee Ti-Yi-Yo

C POSITION

Use after INDIANS (page 24).

Ensemble Parts 1–4
Suggested Sounds: 42 **Part 1** *Synth 1/Funny Vox*   **Part 3** *Synth 1/Glasses*
   Part 2 *Organ/Accordian*   **Part 4** *Synth 2/Oboe 2001*

Barrel of Monkeys!

G POSITION

Ensemble Parts 1–4

Suggested Sounds:

Part 1	*Wind 2/Sax 2*	**Part 3**	*Wind 1/Flute 2*
Part 2	*Wind 2/Clarinet 2*	**Part 4**	*Bass/Slap Bass 1*

Boogie-Woogie Goose

C POSITION

Ensemble Parts 1–4
Suggested Sounds: **Part 1** *Brass/Trumpet 1*   **Part 3** *Wind.2/Clarinet 1*
                      Part 2 *Brass/Fr Horn 2*   **Part 4** *Brass/Trombone 1*

On With the Show!

C POSITION

54

Use after THE KEY OF G MAJOR (page 42).

Ensemble Parts 1–4
Suggested Sounds:

Part 1 *Organ/Elec Org 2* **Part 3** *Strings/Pizzicato*
Part 2 *Strings/Harp 2* **Part 4** *Strings/Cello 1*

HAND POSITION:

LH plays lower tetrachord
RH plays upper tetrachord

Three Wise Monkeys

KEY OF G MAJOR
Key Signature: 1 sharp (F♯)

Allegro moderato

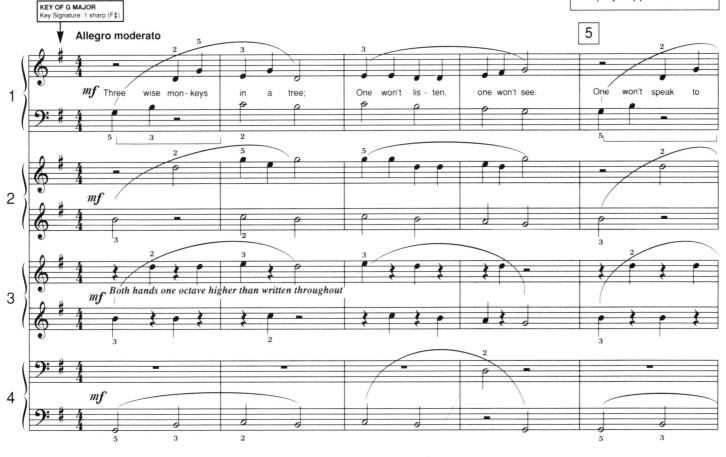

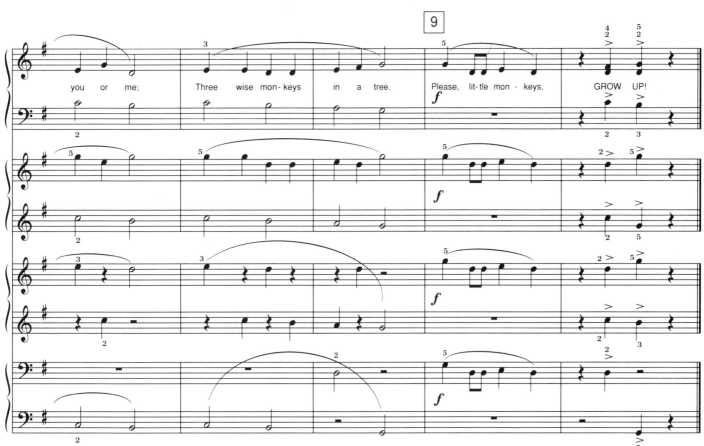

Use after WHEN OUR BAND GOES MARCHING BY! (page 46)
or with the beginning of LESSON BOOK 2.

Ensemble Parts 1–4
Suggested Sounds:

Part 1 *Special/Shakuhachi*   **Part 3** *Special/Whistle 1*
Part 2 *Special/Koto*   **Part 4** *Special/Bottleblow*

The Caravan